Light at Point Reyes

poems by
Joan I. Siegel

For Lucille & St...
Much love
and best wishes...
Joan
(11. 25. 12)

Light at Point Reyes

ISBN 978-0-9853151-1-5

Cover photo by Emily Solonche
Cover design: Jack Heller
Book layout and design: Kimberly Martin

Published by Shabda Press
Post Office Box 70483
Pasadena, CA 91117
www.shabdapress.com

For My Family

Acknowledgments

(Some poems listed below may appear with different titles and in altered form since publication.)

Alaska Quarterly Review	"Distant Light"
	"When My Father Stops By"
Amicus Journal	"Drought"
Atlanta Review	"First Song"
	"Three Lost Boys"
Calyx	"Bitter Fruit"
Carolina Quarterly	"Boogeymen"
	"Au Pair"
Commonweal	"At Rashad Phychiatric Hospital"
	"Interim"
	"Letter to My Mother"
	"Nesreen in Baghdad"
Connecticut Review	"Chinese Calligraphy"
	"Orpheus"
	"Patience"
	"Photo: My Grandmother from Minsk"
	"Playing *The Moonlight Sonata* in Late October"
	"Wilderness Camp"
Cutthroat	"After Love"
Free Lunch	"Afghanistan"
Hampden-Sydney Poetry Review	"Questions"
	"After the Storm"

Hawaii Pacific Review	"Soap"
Ibbetson Street Journal	"Driving Home from Ithaca after Leaving My Daughter at College"
JAMA	"Infertility Clinic"
	"You Dreamed You Had Two Hearts"
Margie	"First I Leave Home"
New Letters	"Sometimes When I'm Walking on the Street"
Nimrod	"In the Women's Gallery"
North American Review	"Der Tod der Musik"
On Earth	"First Crocus"
	"To a Dead Owl on the Roadside"
Oregon Review	"O'Keefe: Abstraction—White Rose No.3"
Poet Lore	"In Late November"
Poetry East	"Dance"
	"Holding My Daughter's Hand"
	"On the Voice Recorder"
Prairie Schooner	"Mother & Daughter"
Raritan	"In the Living Room of the Woman without Daughters"
San Jose Studies	"After the Funeral"
Southern Humanities Review	"Child Bride"
Southern Poetry Review	"Monarch in Late Autumn"
West Branch	"Penelope"
Witness	"Exile"
Zone 3	"Last Song"

The author is grateful to the editors of publications in which these poems first appeared as well as for the generous support of Joel, Emily, Susan and Jack Heller, Chase Twichell, William Trowbridge, Diane Wakoski, Rita Gabis, Mary Makofske, Djelloul and Marilyn Marbrook and her editor, Teresa Mei Chuc.

Contents

PART I

Abstraction—White Rose No.3
(Georgia O'Keeffe)

White tip of desire
hot as the glassblower's rod
this incandescence.

Last Morning of My Mother

wears my mother's face. One eye
half closed, unfinished
with memory and light,
unready. How otherwise to be?
Three long days. Three nights.
Like the bird that once mistook
my window for the sky,
one eye looking

Later

We'll pass along this road to find
the house painted another color, hear
different music.

    Gone the wood thrush, whistling
swallow. Someone else bending among
our peonies, lavender, wild creeping
thyme.
                Stones rolled away
where we buried the cats. Gone
the cherry tree, branches
a white cloud outside the window where
light thieved in.

Infertility Clinic

I call you from darkness
where you have waited
all my life like a thought
before the words
that name it. I name you
Daughter.
    I want to plant
the ripe grain of you
in my earth   carry
you through seasons
to your first springtime
when your eyes open to a green
world where moths flower
beside dandelions and songbirds
returned from rain forests
singing your birth.

Bitter Fruit

She climbed up
on her father's lap just before
he died of influenza in 1917.
Her mother blamed her.

She remembered ironing
her red wedding dress,
how no one cared
she didn't wear white.

She remembered lying on a couch
after a miscarriage, how years later
they tied her legs because the doctor
was late when I needed
to be born.

She had two pianos
she gave away
the one
with the sweeter tone.

First Crocus

Crouched
in darkness
all winter
like Prosperine
presses upward
against stones
hairy fringe
of roots   soft
indulgence
of worms   cracks
open earth's rimed
cellar door to this early
April sky   shivering
unfolds itself...still
wearing the purple
stain of Hades.

Distant Light

Three bright points
of a triangle shine
outside my mother's window:
Venus, the moon & a star
whose light set out
seventy-two years ago
she was a girl
drinking from a glass
at the kitchen table thinking
about a boy in her class while
her mother hung laundry
screech
of the clothesline
the boy
leaves blowing in St. Mary's Park
taste of milk.

Eclipse

Illusion, this moonlight
that isn't light of moon.
Mere sleight of hand
like making a penny disappear.

Still amazed, we hold
our breath while earth holds
in darkness. Lose
our balance. Reach

for each other despite all
we know of magic,
physics, molecules
that never touch.

In Late November

You look up
from what you have been
doing all day, notice
the angle of light diminishing
around you and on the trees shorn
of their October radiance
on the flanks of the gelding
and mare grazing in the field where
shadows slide like hour hands between
blades of grasses to your hands
on the window sill, you put down
what you are doing because the days
are shorter now, the last waves
of starlings, wheeling of vultures
and crows have passed, black cat
gone missing, both horses need
a walk before dark.

Falling Asleep to Bach's Partitas

late afternoon four days short
of winter solstice the cat
insistent I nap curls
in the curve of my body   two paws
burying my hand in her belly
thick fur half awake my palm
counts heart beats counterpoint
to Bach's andante diminishing
in cadence with light outside
the window inside darkness
again some long ago winter
afternoons falling asleep someone's
hands covering me with a blanket
my mother playing the piano
the heart's metronome
keeping time.

Last Song

The room grew dark, darker than it was
as clouds gathered across my mother's eyes.
The sky hung soft as fleece in the silver birch.
The wind cried, she whispered.

As clouds gathered across my mother's eyes,
I opened the windows wide and sang because
the wind cried. She whispered,
We are those ancient songs you sing.

I opened the windows wide and sang because
she touched my face, her fingers pale as milk.
We are those ancient songs you sing,
her lips parting to let the breath come out.

She touched my face, her fingers pale as milk.
I promised to sit with her all night and sing.
Her lips parting to let the breath come out
as she closed her eyes and let the moon come in.

I promised to sit with her all night and sing.
The sky hung soft as fleece in the silver birch
as she closed her eyes and let the moon come in.
The room grew dark, darker than it was.

Letter to My Mother

Early October sky wears more gray
than your old wool sweater. Wind chills
my neck like the string of pearls left
on your dresser.
    Three months since
we shoveled earth's dust into that windless
hollow where you waited for sky
to close, wind to worry our hair, rattle
branches as you turned to undoing.

    What is left of you, intangible
as music left sounding in the flute, dissolved
in the wind and its ways. Intangible
as shadow that waits to unthread memory,
bones— renders us chill as your face that shocked
my lips when I bent the last time
to kiss you good-bye.
    I pulled back leaving
you un-kissed who had become some other thing
already, one of the elements—
    Fire. Earth. Water. Wind.

PART II

My Daughter Learns to Write Chinese Calligraphy

Between three circling fingers
and the balancing thumb

she anchors the brush
in her right hand. Obedient,

the left hand rests. She shapes
bristles on the ink stone— hairs

sparrow-beak sharp. She paints
the first descending

stroke for *sky.* She lifts
the brush. Draws a pair

of wings. Last, the right
falling water-drop stroke.

Her back is straight as bamboo.
Her feet are silent under the table.

Sky dances in black tights across
a field of rice paper.

First Song

Did the voice rise a cappella in answer to wind's
cold piping through a shaft in the cave? Staccato

as bird song beyond tundra or pulled wire-
thin, whine of ice rubbing on ice? A baritone

rumble of distant thunder or woody as new mother's
cooing? Keening to the child born dead?

Did he croon to himself who sketched in red and
yellow ochre an epic song of bison, aurochs, horses, deer?

Oratorios of winter, stealth, blood? Incantations
taut as gut stitched through animal skins? And did

bellows of the cave roar in answer, bass
canonic voices sturdy as mammoth bones?

On the Voice Recorder

The pilot sings to himself
at the hour of death   first song

of his mother's voice that eased
him as a boy when darkness

welled— only her voice
again and again from this world.

Playing the Moonlight Sonata
in Late October

There is no moonlight but light
of hickory and ash golden in this steely

afternoon. At the piano my fingers travel
from radiance outside the window, wandering

music as through woods shadowed
by dusk, my mind trailing the path

that rises to momentary brightness, falls
away to deeper tonalities too far

to travel. Loneliest regions of the minor key
where my father went in search of music

when he'd lost his bearings, could no longer find
notes to play. Like Beethoven, leaning heavily

over the sounding board, straining
for music in his head.

Der Tod der Musik

"Instruments caved in with a wild jangle
 of sound..." Franz Mohr, (Cologne, 1943)

When planes came, I raced outside
to watch buildings burn: I watched
fire storming from building
to building, one street to another. I watched
people falling from windows. I watched
people running in streets, flames
drinking their shirts. And when fire swallowed
the Hochschule fur Musik, I heard all
the music that instruments make
when they are dying.

Wilderness Camp

At the front gate I leave
you with the others. Warily
you look back. Already
shadows like black moths
flicker in your eyes. Three pale
fingers slide to your mouth
in the gesture I have known since
that day twelve years ago when
they put you in my arms to carry
you the long way home
from China.
My beautiful
sad daughter
here you will learn
how to make fire
build a lean-to
use a compass

find yourself
whenever you are lost.

Childhood

Reuters Photo: Indian Girl
The New York Times
(April 22, 2001)

When will you come, Monkey God
protector of children swoop
from the mountain   carry
her home?

Eyes scrape the ground like eyes
of a packhorse as she balances
cement bricks on her head.

Ten fingers like reeds.
Seven bricks. Gritty
edges cut her palms.
Her face sags.

One thousand bricks make eighty-six pennies.
How many footsteps make one thousand pennies?
Her mother is ten thousand bricks away.

Why isn't she dancing   ten fingers
clicking   bangles flashing
in the sun? Tonight they will snatch
her pennies. Pocket her sleep.

Holding My Daughter's Hand

Fingers I know by heart when I play
a Bach fugue—

up and down the keyboard,
one imitates the next, slides

underneath, races to catch up, jumps
on its shadow. Each pulling

an invisible thread inside
the mighty warp of keys, weaves

a cloth so transparent—
light shines through.

Picasso: *Child with a Pigeon*

He will remember
softness
feathers
rain.

The heart tapping
in its tight cage.
Bones fragile
as grandmother's
china cup.

Long after
the velvet snap of wings
above the sycamore
wildness
in his hands.

Mute Swan

Milkweed pale
in this morning's
sunshine, three cygnets
clustered beside
her on the mossy bank, she
turns my way.
Reproached,
I see beyond the elegant
neck, white of whitest down
that darkest beauty: razor-edged
wings hammering
to hammer me back.

Stepping into the Photo

I walk with her through the neighborhood
where we were born. Our school, two candy stores,
one Jewish butcher shop with sawdust on
the floor, dead chickens hanging upside down

from iron hooks. She doesn't recognize
my face or know how things turned out. I ask
Who will you be in fifty years? She shrugs
she squints at *fifty* years. Around

our block, we balance on one foot beside
the curb, uncertain why we can't roll off
this earth or saying *mirror* fifty times
it isn't anymore a mirror where

you see yourself and if you stare too long
that person looking back stops being you.

Driving Home from Ithaca
after Leaving My Daughter at College

I listen to Bach's *Art of the Fugue*
winding past old Indian lands   roads
named Chenango   Shindagin   Nanticoke
the river Susquehanna meandering
alongside   the music swells
in longing   warm palliative
to my sadness as Bach wanders
the cosmos solving its perfect
equation   Golden Ratio—symmetry
in sunflowers   face of the tiger   Peregrine's
flight   *harmonia mundi's* whirling
spheres.   At once my daughter
the river Susquehanna   mountains   trees
bunched fist tight   lost tribes—all intersect
counterpoint to the helix of braided
voices spiraling like galaxies
through space   our lives curving
away   to loneliest regions beyond
time's final permutation.

Mother & Daughter
(for my sister)

Not words
you have waited all your life
for her to speak.

What matters
is comforting the body
bathing her
anointing
face
arms, hands
scars on the belly
feet

how it was
after anger had burned itself out
and there was only
the wash cloth in your hand
warm water.

First I Leave Home

Sometimes
things are simply what they are:
a heron's wings unfolding,

a pale stain on my mother's apron
when I was five—
    she was crying
to herself. All these years
I still want to touch her face.

PART III

Each Spring the Wild Cherry

white cloud outside
our bedroom window where
all winter winds shagged
nests   unmooring birds   branches
tangled on a crescent moon.
So many deaths that give way
to this: flowers humming
with the urgency of bees   their honey
seeping into memory lodged
deep in the flesh that makes you
homesick for another place that is
not a place but an earlier time when
it was simply enough to open
your eyes in the white shade
of a cherry tree in full bloom.

When My Father Stops By

This time
he enters without knocking, wears
his old brown shoes. Between moon-
light and his face, leaves rain gold,
orange on pale meadowsweet.

Two Adirondack chairs lean in.
Amazed he sees impatiens bloom
red hot. He won't account for time.
Tell how it feels to be outside
time. Instead he asks about
my mother. *Isn't she with you?*

To a Dead Owl on the Roadside

How did you end up here—
feathers stiff splinters among
this roadside trash?

I have heard your snap of wings   hissing
dive through
darkness.

You who should have grown
old in the deep woods   falling
unheard   full moon spilled

                    from your eyes.

Old Cat

Neither rushing to feed
the body nor
leave it
just yet, lingers
all night into
morning, scanty
coat stiff with dried
excreta, smell
of rot
    letting go
at midnight when balance
fails, green eyes flickering
behind the woodpile: koan
of the body solved.

In the Shelter

first you notice a shiver
along the spine   dog eyes
sucking at your eyes   wary
through the locked
wire crate   telling wearily
his story   how eagerly
he'd paid homage
submitting
heeling
waiting like he was told to wait
head down   legs outstretched on the mat
yet never slavish enough
for the man   not just
the boot
in his ribs   choke
hold of the collar
but
betrayal of dog love
dog love

You Dreamed You Had Two Hearts

The sick one inside your chest.
The other— a spare you carried
in your hand.
It had a key
you kept in your pocket with
your wallet
    a few loose coins.

Patience

I am trying to learn patience
but traffic chokes the city
like the clot strangling
your heart while I step
in place, impatient to cross
the street, walk uphill faster
than I can break through slow motion
elevators to open... close...rise
to the fourteenth floor where
you are not in your room
down in Ultra-sound the nurses say
be patient while morning yawns
into afternoon, the patient's
monitor next door marks
time out of time in my heart
while I study the bent straw
in your water glass, creases
your body patterned on starched
sheets as if they have meaning—
an omen you'd left me to augur.

Orpheus

Years later
you see him in the subway   waiting
for the train to grind up
from the dark— a wrinkled man
out of a story by I.B. Singer:
Wild, white hair. Eyes
rheumy as a sick dog's. Slumped
on one of those plastic benches,
a brown paper bag
a fifth of Wild Turkey
in his hand.

Afterward
he follows
a girl
with that voice   sway
of hips
bare shoulder
an anklet tapping
her heel.

Exile

Once he stopped
an old lady in the park who looked
like his wife   she patted him on the head
told him to go on home.
                   At home
he found a strange woman who wanted
to take off his hat and coat   he grabbed
tight to the coat so she wouldn't
steal it   walked past her to the closet
as if it were the door to his house
in the old country.

Photo: My Grandmother from Minsk

My grandmother from Minsk with the laughing eyes:
a girl nineteen in peasant blouse and skirt,
she holds her first born, my father. It's 1908
as darkness stows away in the seams.

A girl nineteen in peasant blouse and skirt,
she smiles darkly and dark curls crown her face
as darkness stows away in the seams.
That was long ago. Now mother and son are dead.

She smiles darkly and dark curls crown her face.
I remember her papery skin, hair gray as dust.
That was long ago. Now mother and son are dead.
Her first born in her arms and Russia too far away.

I remember her papery skin, hair gray as dust
making me shy with her. But that was long ago.
Her first born in her arms and Russia too far away.
She spoke in Yiddish which I didn't know,

making me shy with her. But that was long ago
in her house. I ate sweet melon with salt while
she spoke in Yiddish which I didn't know.
The salt stung my lips and I could never talk

in her house. I ate sweet melon with salt while
later she lost her words and then her mind.
The salt stung my lips and I could never talk
after she searched the streets for folks she'd lost.

Later she lost her words and then her mind.
One night she struck my grandfather on the head
after she searched the streets for folks she'd lost.
My grandfather died and two nights later she was dead.

One night she struck my grandfather on the head.
My father held them in his arms and cried.
My grandfather died and two nights later she was dead,
my grandmother from Minsk with the laughing eyes.

Sometimes When I'm Walking on the Street

I see an old man wearing your overcoat,
the gray tweed one. He hurries along
bow-legged like you ... I rush to catch
up, call out just when a breeze whisks
the edges of his white hair curling
the same way from beneath one of those
brimmed wool hats you used to wear... I wonder
if the hat blew off his head, would I run
after it, lift it from the sidewalk...hand it
to him? Would I say,
                    I am your daughter...
much has happened.

Monarch in Late Afternoon

Forty million years
this shade of orange, this particular
design in black and green   painted
on wings sheer as rice paper
who flew three thousand miles
just to sit on the edge of this purple
iris next to my house where I am
listening to the last piano sonata
of Beethoven, the one that peers
at darkness through the bright eye
of the world.

PART IV

Drought

This is a season of holding
back. For forty days and
forty nights the sky
will not give. Earth
hardens like a fist.
Even if rain came,
it would roll off the ground like beads
of glass and crack.

The air is mute, dryness
has its own sound
in the brittle grass where
hummingbirds search the dusty
mouths of day lilies.

At night, milkweed
explode
one by one.

Three Lost Boys

In Fargo they wear green golf pants
Florida shirts with palm trees
donated by the Ladies Aid.

        Ten years.
        One thousand miles.
        Ten thousand boys.

They learn to open
a can of soup. Lock
the door.

        Nuer and Dinka children
        wandering with their lives
        between Ethiopia and Sudan.

Downtown
a shopping trip
to Hornbacher's grocery store.

        In the desert so many ways to die:
        Snakes.
        Lions.
        Hunger.
        Thirst.
        Heartbreak.

In the soap aisle
twenty-five brands of soap:
Anti-bacterial.
Deodorant.
Unscented.

                    In the rivers
                    some boys die of drowning.
                    Crocodiles.

Lilac.
Lavender.
Rose.

Afghanistan

Bombs drop on his sleep. Both hands
fall off. Eyes go dark. Sister's
long hair drapes poppies like a web
of finery. Above the rubble
mother's arm sways on its broken
hinge. He feels his way along
steep outcroppings, each bare toe reading
the ground like Braille. Nose guided
by licorice root, coriander, saffron
on the right. Pomegranate, mulberries
to the left. Overhead—starlings, wild
cranes. Swifts scream from the cliffs.

Bogeymen

Toothless in the back alley
every Sunday—*Bubak, Bag Man*
ready to stuff us in his sack, shrilling
Any old clothes? Any old clothes?

Downstairs, *Pooka* in the broom closet
where Mrs. Minogue locked us up when
we were bad—among her mops, soap powder,
Johnnie Walker Black Labels.

Crouched like Caliban in the fusty
cellar storeroom, *l'uomo nero* robed
in his long black hooded coat, impatient
to climb the stairs, rattle our door.

Out back behind the metal garbage
cans and piles of junk, *Moko Jumbie* alert
to our footsteps in the moonless dark
as we dragged the evening trash.

Oh shape shifter most scary—hairy
monster, eater of children like us who didn't
go to bed... *El Ogro...El Coco... El Cuco ...*
we saw you in our closet once trying on our shoes.

Child Bride

*"She called her mother...Her comrades,
but more often for her mother"* (Ovid)

On her wedding night, she cries for her mother.
A bleating sound like "maa."
His hands are tree roots.
His long beard scratches.
It smells.

Payment for her father's debt.
No one protested. No Cyane
to block four black-winged horses
thundering.

A nymph of a girl, this one:
She could be a fountain
of spring water. She sleeps to dream
of sleeping on her mat at home.

In the other story, the mother strikes
a bargain, waits at the mouth
of hell. They go off together happy
through the tender greening until
wheat grows gold.

The Annunciation

"Then Joseph...was minded to put her away privily."
—Matthew 1:19

Was the voice
familiar?

Did light brighten suddenly or
deepen like blood?

A feeling like daydream?

When she looked up
was it still
an ordinary day

clouds bunched above the hills
cardamom and oil
children at the well?

She alone
chosen?

Was she afraid?

Stones
hurled—
the open
pit?

In the Women's Gallery
(Song Dynasty: Fujian Province 1279)

her mother says *pain will make you beautiful*
she soaks the girl's feet in warm water
mulberry root...white balsam to soften skin
alternative to broth of boiled monkey bones

her mother says *this my mother did for me*
We call it "teng" hurting- loving
secret language passed from mother
to daughter shared knowledge of survival

her mother says *"Tuo tan huan gu"*
*cast off old bones to be born again...*she clips
toenails... crushes toes against the sole
sprinkles alum... massages feet

her mother says *you will have perfect 3-inch lilies*
she binds small toes... bends big toe upwards... sews
bindings shut... *this will win you a rich husband*
your mother-in-law's respect

her mother says *put on your lotus slippers...beautiful*
embroidery...each bird each flower. Your husband
will hold them in his hand...his mouth... I know
your feet are on fire... put them on... walk...walk

her mother says *I will beat you...stand... walk*
back and forth a hundred times... do not cry...I curse
you... women suffer for beauty... your feet will be
your face ...walk...daughter...walk...

Nesreen in Baghdad

If I walk and look down at my feet
I will only see my feet walking
on the sidewalk. Then I will know
I am still alive. And the body
of the dead woman in the gutter
is someone else. The stench
I swallow is hers. Not mine.
The wailing is her family's.
Not mine. The car pulling up
beside me is only a car stalled
in traffic. I do not explode:
my blood raining
on the street with scraps of skin
and brains, my lifetime
of molecules housing all
I have ever known—
mother and father
sisters and brothers
my house, my hands
the taste of pomegranates
my nephew's voice
my last thoughts screaming
in widening rings.

At Rashad Psychiatric Hospital
(Baghdad 2004)

They say they'll come back for me
my brothers   I don't trust them
the nurse locks me
in this room   windows
barred like a bird's cage   I sit
on the floor solving the puzzle
of iron bars I tried forcing
apart   bruising my arms purple
where they un-forgave me like brothers
sometimes I fly to a branch
on the date palm to sing
with sparrows   so many
dead from the bombing   bits
of charred feathers drift outside
my window   tiny souls rising
toward heaven with the soul
of my baby sister   mother afterwards
I could not find them   calling
calling their names   mother
baby sister   crushed
in each other's arms under
the roof   I tried to lift
them free   each night the bomb
falls on our house   each night
they catch fire   their souls rising
with sparrows   each night
I find strength   lift
the roof higher

My Polish Grandmother's Citizenship Notebook

This is my right hand.
This is my left hand.
These are my hands.
Those are your hands.
These are my eyes.
Those are your eyes.
Christopher Columbus
came to America in 1492.
The Pilgrims were happy
in their new homes.
George Washington
was the father of our country.
Christmas is a happy
time for every one.
This is my book.
This is my head.
This is my heart.

Soap
(for Ann)

It was simply
a bar of soap
not the brown greasy brick, home-made
of lye and boiled animal fat
but the gleaming white bar scented
with a thousand flowers
from the world before war
before bombs dropped on the vineyard
killing the cow
the plane so close
she could see
the pilot's jeering face
she and her baby brother pulling
their mother out of rubble
how many nights the pilot fell
into her dreams laughing
while dead cow stood up to look around
with soft eyes   even after war
she was fourteen on her bicycle
three soldiers   their hands
pulling plying sudden cry
of the startled sparrow in her throat
arms   legs flying
home...mother placed in her hands
a bar of white soap
she held up to the light
stepped into bathwater lathering
foam of a thousand flowers.

Unspeakable
(Ukrainian Survivor WW II)

What words say,
"Soldiers shot them"?

What words say,
"They dug their own graves"?

What words say,
"They didn't shoot babies"?

What words say,
"They tore them apart"?

What words say,
"I survived"?

What words say,
"These words tell you nothing."

Starlings in Early November

I stepped out this morning
into the skirl of starlings

just as a hawk wheeled
above, shocking them

to the sky in a sudden
updraft of dark wind

across the lake, thousands
of black wings beating back

After the Storm

The earth was spoiled forever
in the mouth of the muddy river.
The riverbank slipped and drowned
the lovely willows. Un-moored

in the mouth of the muddy river
dragged and tangled in the roar,
the lovely willows. Un-moored
the king-fishers' nests, the owl's aerie

in the roar. Dragged and tangled
among woodbine, phlox and mallow
the king-fishers' nests, the owl's aerie.
A yellow house with blue shutters.

Among woodbine, phlox and mallow
a black dog on a red barn door
a yellow house with blue shutters.
Ripped from daylight in the churning,

a black dog on a red barn door.
The riverbank slipped and drowned,
ripped from daylight. In the churning,
the earth was spoiled forever.

PART V

Song for the First Born
(for Arwyn)

You ride the last wave
of your mother's dark
sea
drift toward us
one of those puffy white
clouds bearing
good weather.

Tanka

Mere sliver of light
severs both dreamer and dream:
each image dissolves

as the new moon in a cloud
pale cloud in the wind's wide mouth.

Chopin: *Nocturne (Op.27, No.2)*
(à Mme. la Comtesse d'Appony)

To visit heaven
she had only to play it
as written:

dolce & espressivo
rising to
appassionato.

Then gradually
dying away as the breath
of his last words.

Satchmo Plays for His Wife at the Sphinx in Giza, 1961

What riddle does she pose? Stolid woman
part lion, eagle. *What we play is life,*
he says, puts the mouthpiece to his wet lips...
It's been a long, long time... bluesy music coming
up from the throat's deep bottom   spills like moon-
light over her shoulders   breasts   belly
amid the pyramids...this Storyville Anthony
Cotton Club Cleopatra singer-dancer... his music
tellin' her once, tellin' her twice somethin' said
long ago— *You'll never know how many dreams*
...how empty...without you.

Penelope

Who can say
she didn't put down that shroud
more than once
and step into

some lacy wine-dark thing
or a bit of flounce
in tangerine or cool lime

to show off
blackness of black hair
skin sunbathed in Aegean waters
some fluff about the shoulders

collarbones and throat
just enough *décolleté*
and clinging?

Au Pair

Each morning she opens
shutters like a book where she is only
the sub-plot in their story.

On Sundays they sleep late, she dances
barefoot in their living room to the weather
of bells.

Weekdays she steers
their son's pram down ancient streets, past
widows solemn as olive trees.

Mid-afternoon,
Borghese Gardens, the child naps. Nearby
a stone Madonna drapes in moss. Jasmine
blooms. She wonders
how it is to be a nun.

Late above the shining city, night
of lilac and cedar, he kisses all the words
from her mouth.

After Love

I float
as the sky darkens to purple
then black.

A humming
in the feet, legs, thighs,
dark linings,
folds, rises to
belly and breasts
throat—a song outside
my lips.

music with blood in it
from the river.

Magdalene

("By night on my bed I sought him
whom my soul loveth."
—Song of Songs)

The afternoon alabaster
cold. Wind
like wolves'
teeth bites
through chinks
in the wood. Wrapped
in quilts she dreams
she wakes
on altar steps
beneath
the marble
face of Jesus:
wounds healed
chest smooth
eyes sorrowing
he steps down
to her.

Interim

Geese are gone.
The lake creaks
in its tight skin. Air
stiffens, penciled
in birch. Only beech
holds its leaves, copper
earrings that catch
the low pale sun
and shake.

From woods
deer ease up
to the house.

Hunger is harder
than fear. We look
at each other, then
they go back
behind trees
to some place secret
as foxes' dens.

When You Were Gone from the House
(for Emily)

time stopped
with your dolls at tea
the red sock hanging
from your bed.

The house filled with you.

My sadness, indecipherable
as ten blocks circling
a blue crayon on your floor
runic lines you drew
across my book.

I passed from room to room
touched nothing—guardian
of your temple.

In the Living Room of the Woman without Daughters

The stillness is so still
you think all the sounds in the world
went deaf.
       Ten bisque dolls
in white lawn dresses wait out
the summer afternoon. Prim
as doilies.
         Arms awry, fallen
stiff on starched laps. Lips
pursed to speak
or yawn.
       Eyes empty
as teacups.

Questions

My daughter asks me
what she was
before she was.

You were
a feeling,
I say.

You were brightness
on the window shade   light
inside a conch   whirring
of moth's wings
a thought
a word.

She wants to know
what happens to the word after
it is spoken.

A phantom on the tongue,
I say,
it holds.

Vaughn Williams: *Lark Ascending*

This music trails
the darkest place
I go each night to meet
myself, converse among
the dead who teach me all
there is to know.
  Who say
all stories happened once before.

This radiance.

Light at Point Reyes

fog-washed   blurs
boundaries between sky
sea   steep cliff-edges
fall away
to boulders scoured
by tides'
roiling   Bishop Pines
contort   lean easterly
with winds spiraling
upward.
Far off
in warm Baja waters   gray
whales ply the longest
whale-road north   mothers
calves breaching whistling
clicking side by side.
　　My body
vibrates with their song, inner
music, dance—Buddhists
call it *nada.*
　　　　From the light-
house of prisms, refracting
beams sweep darkness.

Dance
(for Joel)

Moon in the white birch
I will dream you
on naked branches
your fingers tap
on our window
wake me to tango
in winter light
lean into your body
arms thrust back like wings
balanced high above
all other sadness.

CPSIA information can be obtained at www.ICGtesting.com
Printed in the USA
BVOW041026151112

305593BV00001B/19/P